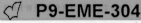
LEARN TO WRITE CREATIVELY BY LEARNING TO SEE.

THE WRITER'S EYE contains more than 100 illustrations which span the vivid spectrum of imagination and suggest new colors for thought. Virtually every school and technique is represented; Leonardo da Vinci, Charles Addams, Richard Avedon, Frank Lloyd Wright, Pablo Picasso, Jackson Pollock, Sir Henry Moore and Herblock are among the many craftsmen who contribute to help the reader see new forms in the familiar patterns of living. The material is selectively divided into sections which examine the facets of man and his environment, offering a simple, stimulating picture-method of learning to write with clarity and impact.

THE WRITER'S EYE

THE NEW VISUAL APPROACH TO THE ART OF EFFECTIVE WRITING

By HART DAY LEAVITT

BANTAM PATHFINDER EDITIONS

Bantam Pathfinder Editions provide the best in fiction and nonfiction in a wide variety of subject areas. They include novels by classic and contemporary writers; vivid, accurate histories and biographies; authoritative works in the sciences; collections of short stories, plays and poetry.

Bantam Pathfinder Editions are carefully selected and approved. They are durably bound, printed on specially selected high-quality paper, and presented in a new and handsome format.

THE WRITER'S EYE
BY HART DAY LEAVITT

DAVID A. SOHN, Editorial Consultant

BANTAM  BOOKS

BANTAM PATHFINDER EDITIONS

NEW YORK / TORONTO / LONDON

RLI: VLM 8.0 / IL 8.12

THE WRITER'S EYE
A Bantam Pathfinder edition / published March 1968

Library of Congress Catalog Card Number: 68-16873

Published simultaneously in the United States and Canada

Bantam Books are published by Bantam Books, Inc., a subsidiary of Grosset & Dunlap, Inc. Its trade-mark, consisting of the words "Bantam Books" and the portrayal of a bantam, is registered in the United States Patent Office and in other countries. Marca Registrada. Bantam Books, Inc., 271 Madison Avenue, New York, N.Y. 10016.

PRINTED IN THE UNITED STATES OF AMERICA

CONTENTS

CONTENTS

"But, Miss Hampton . . . how do I know my ideas are trite? They're new to me!"

"But Mr. Marks . . . nothing interesting ever happens to me, so how am I supposed to write more interesting compositions!"

What does a teacher say to such helpless students:

"Well, don't worry about it . . . just write something down . . . and no excuses on Monday."

"Go downtown and stand on the corner and see if you can't find something."

"Write about something that happened to you that taught you a lesson."

What happens on Monday is that the poor teacher is buried again under a pile of dull themes on the same old dull subjects: "My Hobby" . . . "My Home Town" . . . or "A Trip up Mt. Raspberry." The trouble is that most students don't know where to look for good subject matter. In newspaper slang, they have "no nose for news"; and all good writing is "news." They lack the experience and training to know what will be interesting and important to read, and what will be hopeless.

This book dramatizes the conviction of an experienced teacher that subject matter comes first and always; that much more time should be spent in class and homework in thinking, arguing, and searching for the best material to write about. This conviction is based, not on textbook rules, but on the kind of material which experienced artists have chosen to make people pay deep and startled attention. My conviction is that boys and girls who study such materials during four years of high school will develop a sure sense of what separates bad subject matter from good. Their marks will improve, their understanding will last longer, and they will have more interesting thoughts.

Like its predecessor, *STOP, LOOK, and WRITE!*, this book is based on a visual show, selected and arranged to extend and deepen the power of observation. But this book goes farther into newer worlds of observation and thinking because it uses every kind of visual stimulus: photograph, painting, cartoon, advertisement, sculpture, and diagram. It is an anthology of some of the best work done by great artists in response to what they have experienced.

All writing—student or professional—is a response to experience, so that when students write a story, essay, or poem, they are behaving like the artists whose works are collected in this book. All the way through, students should make continual comparisons between their own responses and what they see in the illustrations. Every picture, drawing, or photograph is good source material for writing. All are the result of an essentially interesting response to the world, either the visible, factual world, or the world of the imagination.

The emphasis here is on "interesting responses," but this does not mean that students are merely supposed to reproduce just what they think is shown on these pages, though that is not a bad exercise in itself. Nor does the selection mean that students should accept as rigid truth whatever any artist appears to "say" about his subject. Students should be free to observe, reject, analyze, accept, describe, or go far beyond what is revealed.

What they are asked to do throughout the study of this book is to SEE, COMPARE, and THINK: then to write about the kind of responses that photographers, painters, sculptors, and cartoonists have put into their work, as against the kind of response an untrained observer might make. There is an essential difference between the image just any-old-body sees looking at a plain girl and what a painter sees.

The book is organized according to a series of universal themes, each labeled with a dramatic word or phrase. These themes, since they are applicable to all people all over the world, have always been the basis of good subject matter—both for writing and conversation —from the time of the Bible and Chaucer to Pop Art and *The Hobbit*.

The twenty themes in this book are separated into four major parts. The first focuses on personal themes, where the emphasis is on writing about individual feelings. The second is more expansive, with stress in composition on the influences of people on people. In the third part, the emphasis changes to relationships between people and things, and other impersonal forces. The last turns to the most intangible of themes and influences, and how they affect man's existence.

The entire book has been planned so that there is a progression from the familiar to the unfamiliar, the more specific to the more general, and the simple to the complicated. If some readers think that certain individual parts do not fit this scheme neatly, they are probably right, since any such plan is to some degree arbitrary. Also, it is part of the premise of the book that students and teachers should find unexpected and controversial ideas for writing, some of them unknown to the author, who is not telling anybody WHAT to think, but WHERE to look.

Throughout the whole "course," one primary style of thinking and observing has been stressed above all: comparison and contrast. All people, but especially students, are confined by narrow observation. Things are seen only in relation to themselves, in isolation; whereas all good writing and thinking is based on noticing and understanding and developing relationships, particularly those that most people don't see. So that such connections may be discovered and used in writing, almost all the images in this book have been chosen in pairs which should be studied together. Also, as students move into the book, they are encouraged to compare images and ideas from one section to another. Ultimately, as the most sophisticated adventure in this kind of thinking, students will be asked to study relationships between different forms of art, especially where the same or a similar theme is treated in different media.

At the beginning of each theme is a brief essay suggesting different ways of studying the images. In some cases definite interpretations of the pictures are expressed; in others possible relationships with life and history are presented. These are all aimed to arouse observation, analysis, and sometimes opposition. Titles, captions, and other information have been included with most images. At the end of each theme are specific assignments for writing, ranging from single sentences to long compositions, and from straight exposition to imaginative fiction.

There will also—the author hopes—be surprises. Some images may not be examples of the themes; some may be very strange examples; some may illustrate ideas close to the theme, but not quite the same. Others have been picked to upset clichés about the subject matter. Everywhere students are expected to look for contrast and conflict, the heart of all good writing.

Some critics say modern youth is too stimulated, and it may be true; but the remark is incomplete. What it really means is too stimulated by the same things: sexy movies, rock and roll, glossy advertising, and too much action . . . it is an Age of Monotony Cults. The purpose of this book is to provide a different stimulus, one that will lead to interesting and dramatic ideas about important subject matter, and eventually to interesting and dramatic ideas about modern existence.

Pre-Test

The following pairs of images are like the first practice sessions for an athletic team or the opening rehearsals for a play. What you discover is important for you and your teacher, since it will reveal what you need to look for later.

Throughout the book the word "image" refers to the paintings, sculpture, photographs, and drawings which the artists have produced. The images range from fairly literal representations of what the artist actually saw in real life, to fanciful representations of what he "saw" in his mind's eye. This contrast will be revealed in the first two pictures. It is also important to keep in mind the fact that a concrete image on paper can stand for abstract ideas and feelings of the most intangible and controversial kind. In this sense "image" means "symbol."

Perhaps you have not had much experience in comparative observation and thinking, especially in relation to the visual arts. But in the experiment that follows, the point is not to worry about the newness of the writing exercises, but to go ahead and find out what you can do.

Study the first pair of images, both singly and comparatively, and then cover up one and write a brief composition about what you see in the other, and about your reactions to what the artist has produced. Then reverse the process. After letting these two compositions sit for a week or so, away from your attention, study them again and write a somewhat longer composition comparing the two pictures from as many points of view as seem important to you.

Ideally, you should keep these first papers for future reference, to look back upon and compare with the kind of writing you do later as you go through the book. At the end, you might return, study the pre-test again, and write several new compositions, to see how your powers of observation have changed.

Trio for Three Telephones

Part One:

MAN AND HIS OWN NATURE

The themes in this first part are based on human feelings: Love, Fear, Pride, Loneliness, and Courage. The major emphasis in text, images, and exercises is on these primary emotions as they are felt by a single person— either within himself or in relation to one or two others. In some cases, the stress changes to include the individual emotion as it is associated with things, like animals and games; but essentially Part One focuses on man and himself.

As you look at these pictures, answer the following questions for the development of your compositions: What emotion is expressed in the image? How intense is the feeling? What variations of the basic emotion do you see in each section? What kinds of action has the emotion aroused? What is the virtue, or wrongness, of the emotion revealed by the images in the picture?

In comparing the pairs of images, it is often important to consider what caused the emotion, for this may control the overall course of what you say. Specifically, it may be vital to stop and analyze causes when you feel in the mood to express violent opinions. Someone in a picture, especially if it is an old one, may look "stupid" to you until you understand what may have provoked the emotion.

Titles or captions are given in most cases, not to tell you what to write, but to start you thinking. Important facts are included too for some images. Both may be important if you try to determine the artist's purpose in painting his picture, making his sculpture, taking the photograph, or drawing the cartoon.

The first theme begins on the opposite page, with a quotation and a first image to suggest ideas. On the next page is a brief essay introducing certain ways of studying. On page 26 are the first exercises for writing.

First Theme:
LOVE

*Though I have the gift of prophecy,
and understand all mysteries, and all knowledge;
and though I have all faith, so that I could
remove mountains, and have not love, I am nothing.*

I Corinthians, 13

The Love Goddess in America

"O, my love is like a red, red rose" . . . "Love is the sweetest thing" . . . "Frankie and Johnnie were lovers" . . . "What is this thing called love?" . . . "Love is not love which alters when it alteration finds" . . . "The Definition of Love.". . .

Is there any such thing as a "definition of love"? Is there a special kind of emotion known and accepted as Love, infinitely more desirable than Hate? Or are there simply different kinds of love, as the old phrase suggests: "Sacred and Profane Love"?

The paintings, photographs, and the drawing in this section were chosen partly on the basis that they suggest different kinds of that classic emotion. One general assignment is to write about "kinds," with the idea of trying to express in words, where it is humanly possible, how each image illustrates the general theme of the whole group, and varies from the others.

It may be that a perceptive observer will decide that a specific image, say the picture on page 21, has nothing whatever to do with love, that it is a different kind of emotion altogether. Then an argumentative composition could be written explaining why.

In relation to any of the images here, it would be appropriate to write purely descriptive essays on the feeling or spirit of what is shown, suggesting rather than explaining how it relates to the general theme.

In making comparisons and contrasts, there will be obvious ways of associating two facing images, and these may make for good writing; but do not be carried away by first impressions. Two images that appear quickly to be quite different may reveal interesting, subtle likenesses.

After studying pictures, students sometimes ask: "What are we supposed to see and write about?" There are no regulation things you are "supposed" to see. Write what you think as an individual, no matter how unusual. Just be prepared to refer to details in the pictures to show what you mean.

Korea

·LIFE·

His Mother: HERE HE IS, SIR

Ideas for writing:

1. Which pair of images reveals the greatest contrast? Explain why.
2. Which pair suggests likenesses that are more important than differences?
3. Write single-sentence definitions for the various kinds of love—or devotion, or adoration—revealed by the images.
4. Do you think any one of these images has nothing to do with the main theme or suggests, perhaps, the wrong kind of love?
5. Do you think another word or phrase would be more suitable than "love" for certain images? Why?
6. Write a purely descriptive essay suggesting the mood or atmosphere of any one of the images. Do not use any words like "love" or "devotion."
7. Write an explanation of why you think one of the artists did what he did. Develop your reason by referring to very specific parts of the image.
8. Can you write a full comparison between any of these images and one you have seen somewhere else? Or between one of these and a movie, TV play, book, or scene from actual life?
9. Which picture contrasts most sharply with all your associations with the idea of love?
10. Write a brief dialogue, incident, or stream-of-consciousness essay to fit one of the images.
11. Make up new titles for the images in this section, and in the rest of the book. Write satirical or funny ones, if you like.

FEAR

... why do I
yield to that suggestion,
Whose horrid image doth unfix my hair,
And make my seated heart knock at my ribs,
Against the use of nature? Present fears
Are less than horrible imaginings.
My thought, whose murder yet is but fantastical,
Shakes so my single state of man that function
Is smothered in surmise, and nothing is
But what is not.

Macbeth, Act 1, Scene 3

The Cry—Edvard Munch

What are people afraid of? injury? loss of face? insecurity? opposition? not being able to win?

Is there any difference between fear and hate?

Or is the best answer that people are afraid of what they do not know?

In some of the images in this section, the causes of fear are obvious, so that the important element to study is the emotion the person is experiencing. What does it make him look like?

In other cases, where there is no clear cause, imagine a situation that might have started the fear. Keep in mind this most important question: Is the reaction revealed in the picure what could be naturally expected by such people under such circumstances? Be sure the ideas, feelings, and language you choose are justified by the evidence in the images.

In addition to the usual comparisons and contrast within pairs of images, you might also study the whole set, to see whether any one aspect of fear is outstanding. Or does any group of three or four suggest a common characteristic?

Head of a Lost Soul—Michelangelo

The Face of Fear

Mouths—José Orozco

Watson and the Shark—J. S. Copley

Ideas for composition:

1. Which of these images is closest in spirit to your own experience of fear?
2. In some of these pictures, the cause of fear is perfectly clear, as in the painting of the shark. In which others is the cause most ambiguous? Explain what you think caused the reaction pictured?
3. Edvard Munch's lithograph "The Cry" is most like which photograph or painting?
4. Orozco's lithograph "Mouths" is most like which other image?
5. Do you think the two images on pages 32 and 33 should have been placed opposite each other in the same section?
6. Is Snoopy's attitude like human beings? Or is it merely fanciful?
7. Of all the details in these pictures, which is the most effective in revealing the essence of fear?
8. Do any of these images suggest what happens to fearful people when they are not alone?

PRIDE

Pride goeth before a fall-out.

Anonymous

Pride is two-faced. To describe one aspect of it, you pick words like "proud," "confident," "sure," and "poised." For the other, you use words like "arrogant," "conceited," and "cocky."

Which meaning you use depends mostly on how someone's actions look to you in your private, wishful mind. It is not a matter of proof. An action or an expression or a gesture which you think is conceited may be openly admired by someone else. A child's pleasure in his own performance is amusing to some: others think "There's a kid that needs to be cut down to size." Many teachers are especially allergic to any student who shows his belief in himself. He can have pride, but he must not show it.

Pride is particularly embarrassing in a democracy, where anybody is supposed to be as good as anybody else —at least in theory—with the result that the older you grow the less you show what you feel even if you honestly know that you are justified.

All the images in this section can be discussed in relation to this central conflict between "pride" and looking "too proud." In musical terms, the pictures are variations on a theme, and this is one good starting point for studying the whole series. What is the variation, how big is it; and what does it prove?

But there are other beginnings too, as the writing assignments will show. What, for example, is suggested about the subject's own attitude toward his pride? That is, where is pride least self-conscious?

Ideas for writing:

1. Describe one image from the point of view that the subject appears too proud for his own good. Do the same one from the opposite point of view: that the pride is quite justified. Explain fully what you see in the pictures to justify the two attitudes.

2. Write the same contrast, but in a very indirect fashion: reveal thoughts and feelings in the subject so as to make the reader feel the conflicting emotions—confidence or snottiness.

3. Imagine that the subject has just finished a speech to a particular audience. Go back and make up the speech so as to reveal the spirit of the speaker. Or you might imagine that the speaker has just said something important to a son, daughter, lover, or relative. Such a composition would be like the dramatic monologues of T. S. Eliot, Robert Browning, or Robert Frost. When you are finished, study your work from the point of view of the question: "Does my diction and phraseology fit the atmosphere of the image?"

4. Which two images are closest in spirit, and which farthest apart?

5. Choose two pictures which you think should have been paired for comparison and contrast, and explain your reasons.

6. In which picture is the subject amused at his own pride, and in which quite serious and intense? Give evidence from the image.

7. What effect does the other person have on the one who is proud?

The Old Guitarist—Picasso

In the face of the ferocious modern campaign for togetherness, it is a strange question to ask whether there is any virtue in being alone. Maybe it is even more grotesque—in these hoarse and bugging days—to ask whether there is any possibility of being alone again.

There are so many people—with more coming—and so many cars, and so many laws and restrictions, and so much noise from horns, telephones, TV, and Musak, that a moment of silence is rather frightening.

And yet, the other day, one teen-ager said that she liked the blasting thunder of a discothèque because it shut out everything else in the world so that she could be alone. She certainly has no intrusion from her partner, who is twenty feet away. Here is a kind of alone togetherness which seems to be very satisfying, and may be an answer to the dilemma posed in the first paragraph.

Perhaps young people are rehearsing for the later battle they will have to fight against all the people who want to invade their private lives: state agencies, federal bureaus, poll takers, throwaway mail addressed to "Occupant," and "every-member canvassers." If this should work so that teen-agers can retain their sanity and sympathy in an overgrown society, they may have begun to find one answer to what Robert Frost called the worst problem of the future: "How to crowd and still be kind."

The pictures in this section make up a kind of pictorial essay on the ancient battle between privacy and public relations. They do not give any clear answer, but they rather dramatize the atmosphere of different realities: lonely and alone.

The Bearing of the Cross—J. Bosch

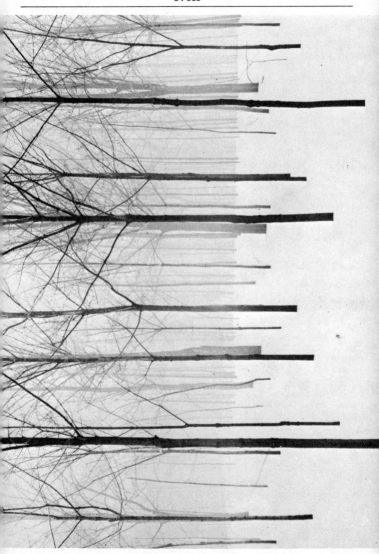

Young America, 1950—Andrew Wyeth

Exercises for writing:

1. For which of these images is "loneliness" the right word? Why?
2. Which of these situations would you rather be in, alone? Why?
3. Which situation is most realistic?
4. Which most romantic?
5. Discuss the words "lonely" and "alone" in relation to the pictures with more than one person.
6. Describe the spirit of each image by a single sentence containing a simile or metaphor.
7. Describe the relationship between one solitary figure and his background. What effect does this background have on the picture as a whole?
8. Despite the lonely aspect of some images, there may still be a sense of communication with something not shown. Which image has this quality most emphatically?

Fifth Theme:
COURAGE

... the soldier, ...
Seeking the bubble reputation
Even in the cannon's mouth.

As You Like It, Act 2, Scene 7

The Flying Codonas—J. S. Curry

Courage is often just a matter of imagination. If you don't imagine what dangers lurk about you, you can be a hero without really trying. But if you do imagine things, you may have to work just as hard controlling fear when you climb a high ladder as a soldier does when he goes out on patrol alone.

The trouble is that courage doesn't mean the same thing to all people. You may think that anyone afraid of high places is ridiculous, whereas patrols are the real thing. This is empty, standardized thinking, or non-thought: the observer sees only the situation, not the person caught in it. This narrow view is one reason why adults push their children too far too fast. They are concerned about general areas of activity rather than specific human beings.

Some readers may think that one or two images in this section have little to do with courage. In these cases, the observer should think of the particular individual in his situation, not someone else in another situation.

Another way to look at courage is to think of the reasons people do apparently crazy things. Why in his famous old comedy "Safety Last" did Harold Lloyd not hire a double to take the chance of falling, or why didn't he use trick photography? Why didn't the young Israeli violinist, crippled by polio, quit? Why do people go on lion hunts?

These questions are all important in an era swamped in security. Probably nobody could make a movie today entitled "Safety Last": too many agencies would protest. Also, it would go against the great contemporary slogan: "I'm not going to stick *my* neck out!"

Study the images in this section from the point of view of the emotions which the individuals appear to be feeling in the face of obstacles and dangers. These suggested feelings may really tell you something important about courage.

"We regret to inform you . . ."

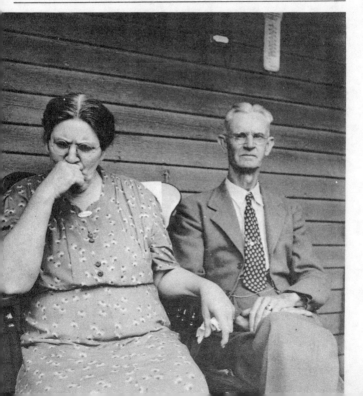

Exercises for writing:

1. Which image seems to you to have the least to do with courage? Explain why. Then write a second essay showing why the individual may have been acting very courageously, given his particular nature.
2. Contrast two images as showing very different kinds of courage.
3. What would make you take the same risks as Harold Lloyd, or "The Flying Codonas," or the lion hunters?
4. Narrate an incident in which you overcame fear and proceeded to do something that others thought was courageous, or that others thought was silly.
5. Describe your emotions at a moment of great danger.
6. Did you ever see anybody do a cowardly act? Describe it and your reactions at the time, and now, if they are different.
7. In which of these pictures do you think group courage was more important and powerful than individual feeling?
8. Explain how one image shows an outward appearance almost completely opposed to the idea of courage.

Part Two:
MAN AND OTHER PEOPLE

Now, you have to cope with a larger world, where the individual is aroused or limited by more and more people. Problems of observation and thinking become more complex because there is more to notice, and the conflicts and other relationships have become thicker.

At first, these are near, as in the opening theme which is based on the Family; and some of the connections may seem obvious and well-known. But look closer, for these artists often see something very special about the obvious. Or they may not be "talking" about the obvious at all.

In each image, even if only one or two people are shown, students should look for the forces in a crowd. People may be highly organized with special rules, as in some of the images in FUN AND GAMES, or they may be loose and variable, as in MAN APES HIMSELF; but "they" are always there, full of force and fight. One of the best subjects for writing is the way a single individual is turned on by the attitudes and acts of a large group. Does the image suggest loss of identity? Or you might argue that it isn't a loss; it is the way he finds his identity.

This whole section raises problems of morality as dramatized by the visual appearances of the world. Do people settle these problems by determining for themselves what is good or bad, or do they simply go along with the crowd? Later sections will focus on standards of judgment that come from more impersonal and abstract sources.

Finally, since there is so much to see and think and write about, you may find that you will have to be more careful of the form and organization of what you write. Order will become more important, especially what you say first and last. Since you can't possibly say it all, you may have to limit your writing much more positively to a single clear conclusion.

First Theme:
THE FAMILY

Americans have been for so long brought up on the idea of the sanctity of the family—"The family that prays together stays together"—that it is almost impossible for them to imagine the State having anything to do with it. In their secret hearts, Americans are sickened by the thought that someday their children might be turned over to the government for any kind of training, as in Russia and China.

There are other powerful convictions about the family which have been so ingrained in people—and not just Americans—that they are like myths: universal, unalterable truths. Some appear engraved in public and hackneyed words, and woe to anyone who defaces them: "A boy's best friend is his mother." In fact, it might be said that the family is the oldest and biggest cliché in the world.

For many centuries no one questioned these clichés, these "truths." No one ever thought about them or discussed them, really. They were just there, like the weather, and everybody acted accordingly. Now, however, many are being questioned and investigated, and controversial reports are being published, particularly in the big circulation magazines for young adults. Study groups are being formed to discuss "the family," and courses are being added to school and college curricula.

The images in this section say and suggest many ideas about the family. Study them carefully in relation to each other, in relation to what you have been taught, and in relation to what you have heard, read, and experienced.

Mother and Son—Rudolfo de Luca

"Gee, Dad, what I want is a father, not another pal."

Exercises for writing about THE FAMILY:

1. Which image in this series is the worst cliché? Why?
2. Which image is the strongest and most important variation on an ancient idea? Why?
3. Explain any important connection you can make between one of these images and your own experience.
4. Which image seems farthest away from your own experience or from what you have heard?
5. Take any famous line about the family—"Be it ever so humble, there's no place like home"—and show how a visual image here compares with it.
6. Many people, on seeing a strange or grotesque work of art about a familiar or friendly subject, are likely to react violently: "How ridiculous!" If one of these images provokes such a feeling from you, stop and think it over and then explain just what you mean by "ridiculous."
7. In any work of visual art, the artist uses certain tricks and devices to make one feeling stand out against another. In your own words—do not worry about artistic terminology—show how emphasis and subordination are achieved in one image.
8. Describe one of the pictures in purely emotional language.
9. Pick one image and explain what you think the artist's purpose was; then show how he chose and arranged his materials to emphasize that purpose.

Second Theme:
FUN AND GAMES

If music be the food of love, play on.

Twelfth Night, Act 1, Scene 1

"Playing" used to mean that you did things easily, not being frustrated about how they might come out. Or, if you did worry, you still knew the result wasn't very serious, as in the world of sports. The line used to be very sharply drawn between fun and work.

Today, life is different, and the word "play" has almost lost its meaning.

In the words of a big-time college athlete: "Look, we don't play football for fun."

This new philosophy dramatizes the paradox. If a game, or anything else, is not for fun, then the word "play" is inappropriate. A new word should be found: harder, more competitive, less cheerful.

A different picture of the same conflict appears in the strange works of the artist Maurits Escher, whose "impossible triangle" decorates page 83. "All my works are games," says Escher, "serious games."

T. S. Eliot once defined poetry as a "superior kind of play," thus adding another note to the discord.

The images in this section play a set of variations on the theme of playing, ranging from the old-fashioned spirit of Snoopy to the modern scientific version at many athletic factories, where football is like a formal course in the college curriculum, with lectures, movies, mimeographed sheets, and textbooks.

The truth seems to be that what used to be fun has become serious, like humor. Perhaps the new generation will double the paradox, making fun of what used to be serious, like sex.

"*Next?*"

Waterfall—M. C. Escher

Exercises for writing:

1. "The Manikin" by Goya was painted nearly two hundred years ago. Does it fit the modern ideas in the introduction to this theme?
2. Do you laugh—way down secretly inside—at the last picture, or should it be taken as a serious marriage between popular music and religion?
3. Do you have any idea what Escher meant by saying that his works, like the one on page 83, are "serious games?"
4. Which two images in this part are most alike, which most unlike?
5. Look up the words "farce," "satire," "sarcasm," and "burlesque" and then show how each one fits a particular image here.
6. Explain why one of these images strikes you as particularly ironical.
7. Make up an idea for a cartoon as close to pure nonsense as Chas. Addams' cartoon on page 82, describe it accurately in words, and then have someone in the art department execute it.

THE NEED TO WORK

My object in living is to unite
My avocation and my vocation
As my two eyes make one in sight.
Only where love and need are one,
And the work is play for mortal stakes,
Is the deed ever really done
For Heaven and the future's sakes.

Robert Frost

"*I'm going to be a computer when I grow up.*"

Men who predict the future often say that in the ideal state, those who do the dirty work will be paid in fat salaries, whereas those who like their jobs will be paid a small amount by the state. The theory is that the latter will have so much fun working that they won't need compensation; joyous jobs will make up for small pay.

Other seers say there won't be any dirty work; machines will do it. Still others imagine a future in which nobody will do any work at all. By then, everything that really needs to be done will be done by pressing a button.

Meanwhile, cars have to be greased, trash has to be carted away, new clothes have to be made, actors have to be found for TV, and people have to be employed to sit behind desks. There are all kinds of jobs around still. Some hate the work, some love it, and for some . . . well . . . "It's a living."

The images in this section dramatize different kinds of jobs, parts of jobs, and attitudes toward work. In some cases the artist has chosen an aspect of work in order to draw a conclusion, perhaps a moral one. In other cases, the image is more objective. Yet even here, perhaps a meaning can be drawn by the observer. Study these pictures from the point of view of what the artist or his work suggests about the employment and those who do it.

Study this section in connection with those on FUN AND GAMES and TECHNOLOGY.

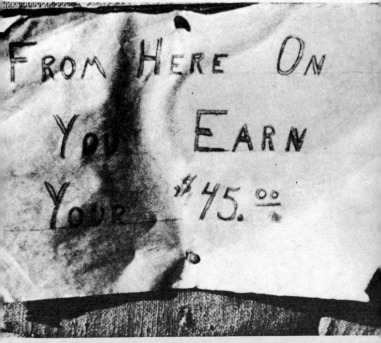

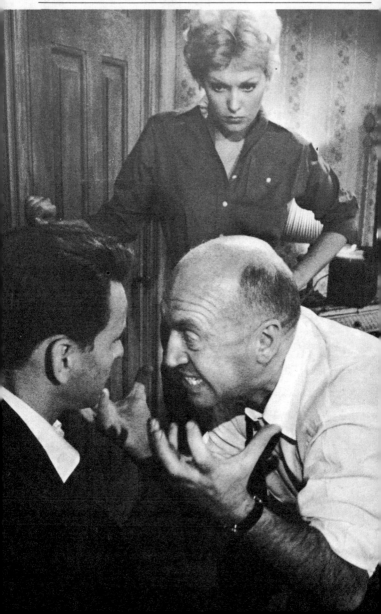

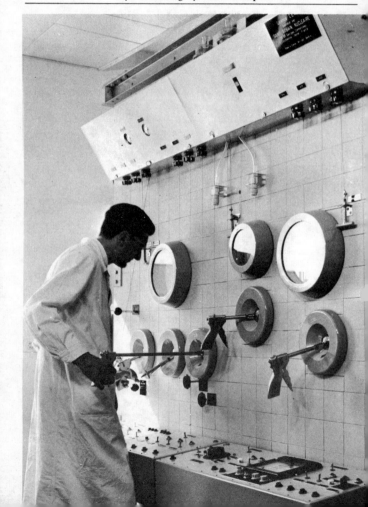

The Banker and His Wife—Quentin Metsys

Exercises for WORK Theme:

1. Choose one picture that shows a kind of work entirely different from anything you know, and explain the contrast thoroughly.
2. Compare or contrast any two pictures as to the spirit of the two jobs.
3. Excluding the first picture, which one suggests the most undesirable job? Why?
4. Which shows the most desirable?
5. Which picture tells you the most about a job of which you know little or nothing?
6. Write a fully developed character study of any of the people shown at work, and include what the picture shows of their attitudes toward what they are doing.
7. Make up a stream-of-consciousness monologue of the thoughts of any of the people portrayed.
8. Write a dialogue between any two people shown.
9. Describe the difficulties, or the conflicts, that any one picture suggests as being characteristic of the work involved.
10. Describe one image in which you see the artist's purpose clearly. Show how details contribute to emphasizing that purpose.

Fourth Theme:
AGGRESSION

"Whaddja expect me to do, turn the other cheek!"

A young athlete who had just been penalized

Red Salute from Korea

This is an age of competition and aggressiveness, dominated by speed, suspicion, and an itch to beat somebody else, once and for all. Some people accept the fury, some want to try to reduce it, and some wonder what lies behind it.

Today there is frantic compulsion to get what you want, RIGHT NOW, before everything is blown up in a tornado of dust. This impulse runs head-on into those equally frantic opponents who don't want you to get what you want, RIGHT NOW. They're afraid that if they hold back, you'll get what they want.

Some students would say that adults provoke aggressive action because they make things take too long, particularly those who still hang onto the antique idea that patience is a virtue. "Nobody," as the slang phrase goes, "buys that act any more."

The belligerent atmosphere is intensified by a general lack of interest in the feelings and opinions of others, especially opponents. This is quite natural in view of the great increase of people who want to be "No. 1."

There is also the curious psychological fact that for many people, not acting quickly and aggressively means losing part of their identity, or status, as it is now called. This is part of the old schoolboy syndrome that makes you feel cheated if you don't trip the guy who tripped you. It goes back to the days of the Bible, when the eye-for-an-eye law was written down.

One way to study these images is to measure the intensity of the aggression in relation to the importance of its cause. Is the result out of proportion, as when you kick a machine that won't work?

To what extent do you think any of these ideas fit the pictures of animals in this section?

Countdown

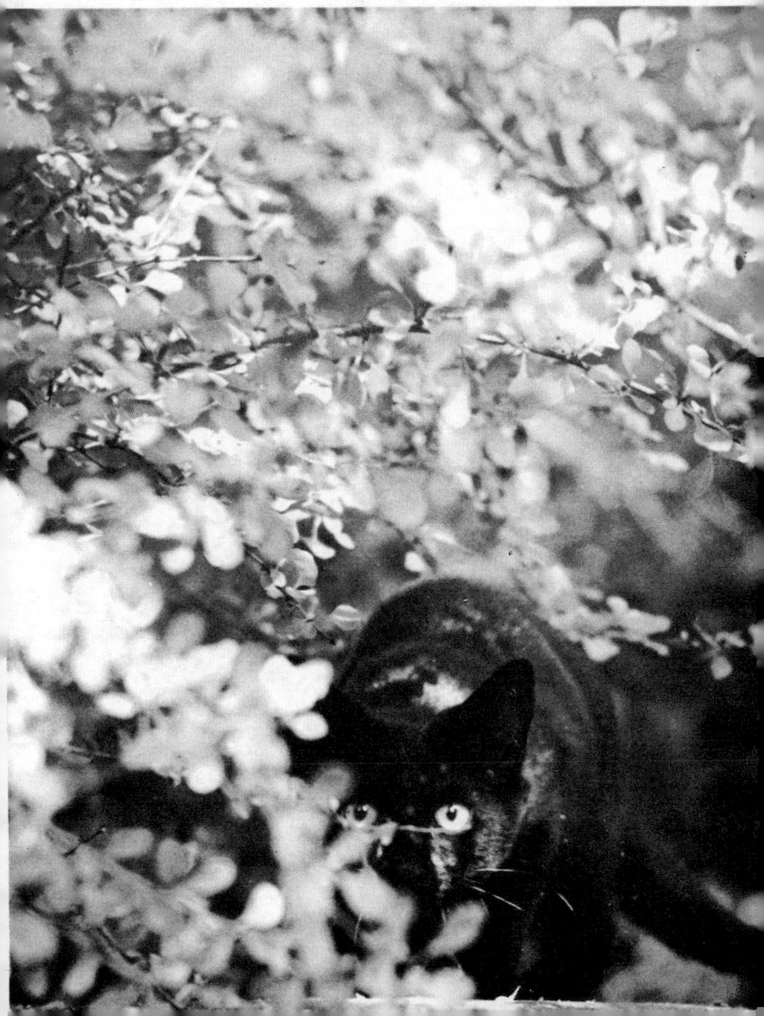

Hogs Killing Rattlesnake—J. S. Curry

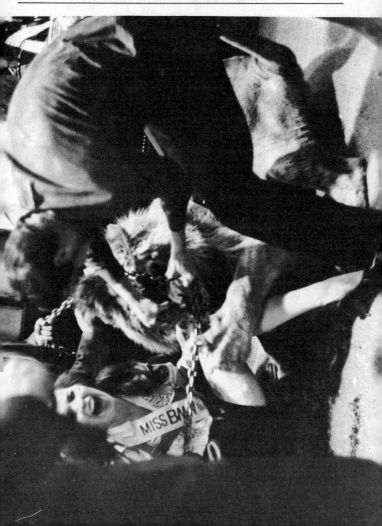

"I hate you!"

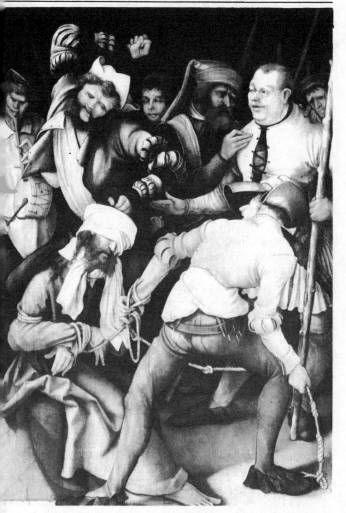

Exercises for writing:

1. Write an essay on the spirit of aggression as suggested by all these pictures.
2. Do you find any surprises in this section?
3. Find an analogue for each image.
4. Pick any one image and describe how it makes you feel, as though you were actually there and were the victim of the aggressive actions.
5. What do you think is the most obvious paradox among these images; and what is the subtlest one, the most complicated, the one that needs the most explanation?
6. Show how in one or two pictures the shapes and forms and shadings contribute to the essential feeling of the whole image.
7. In which of these images is animal behavior most like human, and vice versa? Explain your ideas by thoroughly developed comparisons between animals and people.
8. Compare the effect of aggressive action on other people, as revealed in these images.

107

The history of man is filled with the records of kings, presidents, and dictators who didn't like people to laugh at them or imitate them. They used threats, laws, censorship, and force of arms to stop it; sometimes they succeeded, for a while.

The force of mimicry, however, is so strong that its suppression often boomerangs, revealing the fact that someone is not only taking himself too seriously, but is also trying to inflict that seriousness on others. It may also disclose the fact that someone is trying to cover up secrets that should be known.

How anyone takes imitations of himself is a sure indication of character. The more anyone takes offense—the more insulted he feels—the more pompous he is likely to be, or perhaps the more unsure of his own position. Worst of all, the greater the feeling of offense, the more certainly it reveals that one feels everybody else is wrong and he is right.

And yet imitation, which is sometimes called the sincerest form of flattery, may also be a form of assault and battery. The more acid it becomes, the more it defeats its own purpose. The bitterest and most sarcastic imitations, though they may be right, may perpetuate a wrong by arousing the anger of the victim, not his sense of guilt or a desire to change.

Thus, the most important quality in an imitation may be its temper rather than the sacredness of the thing imitated. The images in this section reveal a wide range in the spirit of the mimicry. Study this quality in relation to the essential nature of what is being imitated. To what extent is the takeoff justified, and to what extent has it gone too far?

"*Winkin' Lincoln*"—Phillip Hefferton

111

Exercises for writing:

1. Which image do you think is the most successful in exposing what should be exposed?
2. Which one do you think would cause the most offense, to whom, and why? What would your reaction be?
3. In what sense is the photograph on page 112 an imitation?
4. As a student, what is your reaction to the picture of the young boy playing King Lear, on page 114? Is there anything in the picture that is unconvincing?
5. The last picture is of a Japanese actor in a very stylized makeup. What is it supposed to imitate?
6. In the advertisement on page 111, compare the commercial imitation with the real painting in the background.
7. Which image do you think is the best combination of exaggeration and truth?
8. Make up and describe an imitation which would be very close in spirit to one of those shown here.
9. Make a speech or stream-of-thought which would be appropriate in spirit to one of the individuals in these images.
10. After precise observation of details, explain why you think the artist reveals his own temper in one of the images.

THE AGES OF MAN

Children may understand their parents, but they never forgive them.

Roman Statue, 1st Century B.C., and Young American

117

As people grow older, into their 50's and 60's, they stare more and more into their mirrors, at the obvious evidence. "But," they say, "I don't feel any different."

Perhaps they are right, and thus are justifiably contented; and yet in a society more and more obsessed by youthful appearances, it is difficult to ignore physical changes. Also, psychological and physiological surveys suggest that even if you think you don't feel any different, you're probably wrong and are fooling yourself with wishful thoughts of "back in my day."

And yet it isn't just the older people who are affected by this conflict of evidence, the internal against the external. Magazines and books are filled with articles on such topics as "What It's Really like to Be 60" (or 40, or 20, or $3\frac{1}{2}$) or "What Is a Teen-Ager?" Maybe even graduate students look into their mirrors and say, "But I don't feel any different."

All the artists in this part have tried to show something of the essence of various ages and of the interrelationship of the ages. One question to consider is what one learns from these individual observations in contrast to studies and polls covering hundreds and thousands of individuals. It would seem logical to say that the latter would prove more; but still one painting, like "Senecio" on page 121, may "say something" of profound importance about oldness, and say it more dramatically and memorably than a house-to-house canvass.

There is also something suggested in these images about how artists have treated age in other times than the present. The older works might be studied from the point of view of whether they represent only a difference in artistic technique or a genuine difference in what they say about age. In this connection, the conflict of ages is vital.

Senecio (Old Man)—Paul Klee

Exercises for writing:

1. Compare two images which reveal a special relationship between different ages.
2. Do you think any picture is false or exaggerated? Why? Develop this explanation by specific references to details in the picture.
3. Can you reconcile the fact that Paul Klee called his painting "Senecio" (old man), and yet drew it to look something like a child?
4. What conflict among ages is most sharply dramatized, or suggested, by one image?
5. Which image is the worst cliché?
6. Which picture, though in part a cliché, has a quality or group of details that keeps it from being corny?
7. What is the greatest similarity among all the images?
8. Does any one of the paintings or pieces of sculpture reveal something you have not noticed in actual life or in a photograph?

Part Three:
MAN AND THE IMPERSONAL ENVIRONMENT

Although the power of human personality is evident in some of the images in this section, most of them suggest physical and massive forces that are infinitely greater than humanity and essentially disconnected from it. Even those that have their beginnings in man can get so out of hand that they become totally impersonal, like violence.

The question is raised here, sharply in some cases, of man's contest with these powers and forces. Sometimes he wins, sometimes draws, sometimes loses; always he is struggling as an individual. Unfortunately, there are some philosophers who argue that the world has less and less place for individual personality and that it is inevitably becoming a more cold and objective place to live.

How many images in this section suggest such a battle and such an outcome? How many suggest changes within ENVIRONMENT? How many suggest that within EN-VIRONMENT itself there are contradictory forces pulling man two different ways at once?

Study all these images from the point of view of what they reveal about the moods, the characteristics of various parts of man's environment. Also, consider what is shown of man's reactions—physical, mental, and spiritual. Finally, after you have seen what those reactions actually *are*, you might express what you think they should be or what yours should be.

The images in this section were chosen as part of a steadily increasing emphasis on the fact that the best subject matter—no matter what kind of writing you are doing—always is rooted in conflict. One of the great weaknesses of amateur writing is that since there is no real struggle involved the reader has little incentive to read the paper through to find out how things come out. No matter which images you choose to write on, think constantly in terms of struggle and outcome.

First Theme:
TECHNOLOGY

The methods of technology are often too complex for most people to try to set down in words, but there are two aspects of this technocracy we live in that the man-in-the-street and the student-in-school can wonder about and write about: the uses of technology and the spirit of technology.

Almost nobody, for example, can discuss the construction of nuclear machinery or weapons—it is even said that the various processes are so complicated that scientists and technicians who work on one cannot communicate with those who work on another because their vocabularies are so ingrown and specialized. And yet the layman can and will talk about the uses of these devices when they threaten to destroy everybody.

The same conflict has developed in the use of less spectacular inventions like TV, automobiles, and outboard motorboats. They are all satisfactory constructions in themselves, but what people do with them is something else.

The other aspect of this theme—the spirit of technology —raises a question for writers: Why have technology and machinery been poor subjects for poetry? During the early years of this century, writers rebelled against "poetic diction" and "poetic subjects," angrily maintaining that anything could be talked about in poetry; and at first, a few did write about anything—airplanes, automobiles, textile machinery, and bulldozers. But it didn't work. The poems were minor and unsuccessful.

In the images throughout this section, do you find any essence of technology which makes it unsuitable for poetry, not merely for a "nature poet" like Wordsworth, but a modern poet like Frost? Are machinery and its father, technology, merely prosaic?

Or, do we need new and different poets?

"*We like it so much, we're making one for ourselves.*"

Three Musicians—Fernand Léger

Intra-Atomic Equilibrium of a Swan's Feather—Salvador Dali

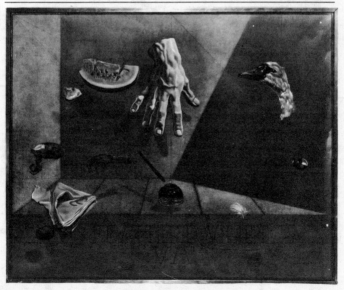

*Forms Arranged According to Laws of Chance—*Jean Arp

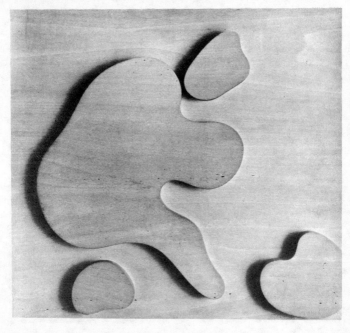

Exercises for writing:

1. Do you think the characters in the first cartoon are ludicrous or not?
2. Write a thorough contrast between the atmosphere of the last two images.
3. Do any of these images, or all of them, suggest any essential relationship between technology and man, not only what it is, but what it ought to be?
4. Do you have any idea what Dali's painting on page 133 means? and its title?
5. Describe the contrasting effect on your feelings of any two images in this section.
6. Compare any image in this section with any other in the book with which it seems to have a distinct emotional or intellectual connection.
7. What do you think the sculptor Arp meant by calling his work on page 134 "Forms Arranged According to Laws of Chance"?

It is not known who started the first argument about living in the country as against the city: probably two Roman brothers who couldn't stand each other. One was elegant and sophisticated, with a love of good talk and tall women; the other was strong and simple and loved to get his hands dirty.

Attitudes haven't changed very much over two thousand years, and the debate still goes on, tritely and impolitely: "The city is a good place to visit, but I wouldn't want to live there" vs. "That's where they pull in the sidewalks at 9 o'clock."

As is always the case in public argument, the conflict appears to be black and white, ignoring the actual facts of the case. There are different kinds of living in the city and different kinds in the country. The city has its worst slums and the country its loneliest farms; the city has the best entertainment—and the worst—and the country has mountains and no traffic lights. Whether the average conditions in the city are better than average conditions in the country is an ambiguous question, as is the worst of the city against the worst of the country. There are even those who like the worst.

For increasing millions of people, the answer to the argument lies in the suburbs, where *some* aspects of city living are retained, along with *some* aspects of country living. But, Suburbia brings problems, too, like MONOTONY, especially in architecture.

The images here dramatize both extremes, and two attempt to build a compromise.

The Kaufmann House—Frank Lloyd Wright

Landscape Near Chicago, 1934—Aaron Bohrod

Exercises for writing:

1. Does any one of these images reveal anything new to you about the battle between town and country?
2. Does any image give what you think is a false idea about town or country?
3. What essential similarity exists between the images on pages 140 and 141?
4. Describe the similarity of atmosphere in the images on pages 142 and 143.
5. What do you think the artist meant by the title "The Mystery and Melancholy of a Street" on page 143?
6. What metaphor would fit the photograph of Mississippi, on page 142?
7. Do you think living in a curved apartment would be any different than the conventional square one?
8. What is an essential contradiction in Bohrod's painting "Landscape Near Chicago"?

Third Theme:

VIOLENCE

Violence is still the sire of all the world's values.

Robinson Jeffers

Atomic Bomb Test

Violence often begins as a specific, personal act, and it may stay there. But like all contagious diseases, and nuclear fission, it has within itself the epidemic possibility of chain reaction, after which it becomes impersonal and undisciplined.

Such an uncontrolled result suggests the moral arguments some people raised against dropping the second atomic bomb on Japan at the end of World War II. Those who now say it was wrong imply that at the time there was a choice over whether to repeat the devastation caused by the first bomb. This speculation is academic in the face of the explanation that the second bomb was let go because "it was programmed," thus eliminating personal responsibility.

Here is the great modern dilemma: will man be able to control the forces of violence which he himself has loosed? Natural explosions, like those in some of the images in this section, have been restricted by planning and invention; but there is a greater challenge in the splitting of atoms and massive rebelliousness. Once they have started, can they be subdued, like floods? Or can they be prevented from starting, like fires?

It is partly a matter of ignorance. In the past, the violent spread of disease was gradually brought under control because man discovered what to do and did it. Now, when the power of universal destruction has been learned, will the way to hold it back be learned in time?

There are attempts under way, on a scientific basis, to study the causes of modern violence, as men have studied and tamed the causes of pestilence and floods. Perhaps someday controls will be established against personal destructiveness, so that it won't blow up and spread until it becomes impersonal and excusable.

The Enraged Swan—Jan Asselyn

Schlieren Photograph of Supersonic Shock Wave

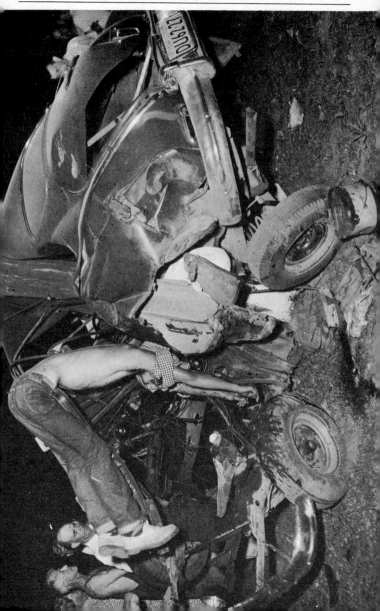

Exercises for writing:

1. Do any of these images teach you anything about violence that you had never thought of before?
2. Think of a particular example of violence, and express it by a simile or metaphor.
3. Compare one of these images to a violent happening in life that you know about.
4. Describe the results of a violent act, both physical and spiritual.
5. Describe the effect of violence on the swan.
6. Retell a violent incident, emphasizing one quality of the explosiveness.
7. Compare the visual effect of the photograph and the actual sound of a sonic boom.
8. Imagine what it would be like to be in the middle of a violent action—like a race riot—and describe your feelings as things happen right around you.
9. What is the difference between the two images of natural disasters, on page 150 and 151?
10. Write a violent speech attacking something or somebody.
11. Have you ever done anything to anybody in a fit of violent emotion? Describe what it felt like, AFTERWARD.

Part Four:
MAN AND THE INTANGIBLES

The themes in this last section present the most difficult problems in observation and writing.

One of the main obstacles is that the essence of the subject matter is abstract and uncertain. Some of the images themselves are definite puzzles, like those on pages 169, 189, and the pair on pages 204 and 205. These will require more concentrated observation, thought, and imagination than any in the book, before you will know what to write about.

Certain ones, perhaps, will be so new to you that they will be virtually unrecognizable at first. Here is where you may have to ask questions, or look up words, or do research on related subjects. It would be wise too to look up material on some of the artists, like Alexander Calder, who is represented on page 193. In this case you should be able to define "mobile" before writing.

Since many works of art are variations on a theme, it is important to look up historical material behind certain images. There have been, for example, many famous statues and paintings on the subject of "Justice," so that a solid expository essay could be made up from a comparison of the sculpture on page 209 with other works from past history.

Most intriguing for some people, and frustrating for others, will be trying to find a relation between the image and realistic human experience, like the pair on pages 200 and 201. Can you explain what either one of these has to do with life as you know it?

First Theme:
MORALITY

The word "morality," which today means "good," has been handed down from its Latin ancestor "mores," which meant popular customs. Literally speaking, this association suggests that what is popular or commonly accepted is good; and anything not customary is bad, or against the "mores," or immoral.

Living would be very easy if "moral" and "popular" were really equal to "good"; but "moral," through years of usage, has also come to suggest "good" according to abstract or religious standards. For many people, commonness and popularity have nothing to do with good; in fact, many common customs, such as gambling and drinking, are still thought of as immoral, or evil. Some religious leaders spend much of their time trying to get the people to stop doing popular things—like dancing and playing cards—and take up better ways of life.

The problem of morality and immorality is also complicated by the fact that what was immoral in one historical time—such as playing games on Sunday—becomes acceptable, or good, or just neutral, in a new time, like today. This makes it difficult for parents and teachers to live with their children. To ease things, some adults try acting like their children, but this often increases the difficulty, as suggested by the cartoon on page 72.

A wave of new morality is beginning to roll in with the idea that it is all right to do anything as long as it does not hurt somebody else, a very practical and American point of view. It is being applied to problems of cheating, drugs, and sex.

The images in this section reflect many aspects of the contemporary problem of morality: change, conflict, harm, and ambiguity. Study them all in relation to what you have been taught, what you believe, what you have seen, and what other people say.

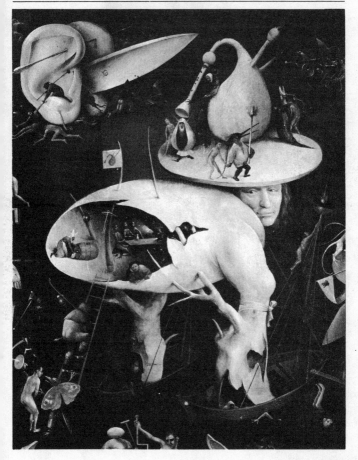

Exercises for writing:

1. Do you think any of these pictures are propaganda? Why? Give evidence from the images.

2. Do you believe in any absolutes of good and evil, or is Hamlet still right: "There's nothing either good or bad, but thinking makes it so"? Discuss this conflict in relation to any of the images here.

3. What attitude in the faces is revealed toward the bribe on page 159?

4. Is the photograph on page 160 a "slash" against the rich?

5. The image on page 161 is part of a large moral painting by Bosch entitled "The Garden of Earthly Delights." One interpretation states that the central figure is a monster from hell with a tavern in his body. On his head is a platform upon which devils are leading sinners round a bagpipe—a symbol of obscenity.

    Show how the word "obscenity" applies to the picture.

6. Do you think the two photographs on pages 162 and 163 reveal any moral attitude on the part of the photographer?

7. On the basis of the photograph and the painting on pages 164 and 165, compare the 1920's with your own generation. Don't wander into corny fields of generalization but stick to what is revealed in the pictures.

8. It has been said that American teen-agers have had such comfortable lives that they do not want to know about the things pictured on pages 162 and 163. Write an essay of your own on this topic.

9. What feelings are revealed by the faces in the picture on page 164?

Second Theme:
FANTASY

*From the conception of **fantasy** as the faculty of mentally reproducing sensible objects, the meaning appears to have developed into: first, false or delusive mental creation; and second, any senselike representation in the mind, equivalent to the less strict use of **imagination** and **fantasy**. Later **fantasy** acquired, also, a somewhat distinctive usage, taking over the sense of whimsical, grotesque, or bizarre image making. This latter sense, however, did not attach itself to the variant **phantasy**, which is used for visionary or phantasmic imagination.*

Webster's Dictionary

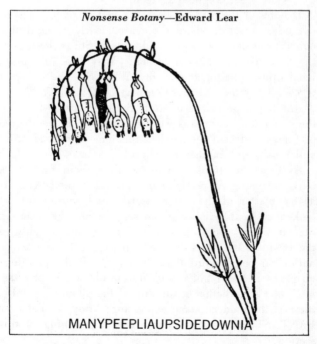

Nonsense Botany—Edward Lear

MANYPEEPLIAUPSIDEDOWNIA

As you consider writing about the images in this section, you might approach each painting or drawing from the point of view of HOW FAR the artist went in representing what he saw in his mind. Is the image so private that it communicates nothing to you at all? Some fantasies do indeed come from people who are almost literally "out of this world."

In the face of such pictures, most people give up: "I can't make head or tail out of that" or "Why don't these artists make people look like people?"

On the other hand, suppose you take a second or third look and begin to consider questions like: "What do these images make me feel like?" or "Is there some meaning suggested by the combination of things in the picture?" or "What was I laughing at, really?"

If none of these ideas work for you, turn to some of the other images, where there are clearly recognizable connections between reality and fantasy. Study these from the point of view of this question: "Why were such unrelated things put together?" or "Why were the two pictures put together, as those on pages 172 and 173?"

Another approach is to study the relationship between the image and the means used to convey it. Is the degree of fantasy affected by the fact that one man used paint and brush, and another a camera?

As these questions suggest, writing about fantasy is partly a matter of personal interpretation; and yet it is also a matter of the use of words, and words may be looked up in the dictionary to see whether the meaning fits the image. Does "grotesque," for example, apply to the extent of the boy's "dream" on page 171? Is "imagination" a better word than "fantasy" for the paintings on pages 172 and 174? Look up the old word "phantasmic" and see whether it fits any of the pictures. Finally, there is the modern slang expression: "Boy, is that ever FANTASTIC!" Is that appropriate to anything in this section?

*Dog Barking at the Moon. 1926—*Joán Miró

"My God, it's following us!"

Exercises for FANTASY:

1. Find one image where reality and fantasy are put intimately together. Describe the effect of this combination on you as an observer. Or, explain what you think the connection means.
2. Try writing a poem to suggest the feelings suggested by one of the pictures.
3. Do you think of any of these "unreal fantasies" as suggesting a "real truth"?
4. Does the dictionary definition of fantasy fit any of the images in this section?
5. Describe some of the basic differences between a painting like Miró's, on page 172, and the "trick" or call it what you will, on page 175.
6. Pick the image you think is the most difficult to understand, spend some time analyzing the question "What is its purpose?", and then see if you can write an answer.
7. Which of these fantasies do you think is the most ridiculous? Why?
8. Write a simile or metaphor to describe several of these images.
9. Express the meaning of one image in terms of a mathematical proportion: "The boy in the 'war game' is to a girl as . . ."
10. Take the image which you think is the "farthest out" and describe it in far-out language.
11. Can you relate any of these images to actual experiences of your own? How?

Third Theme:
BEAUTY

One man's beauty is another man's duty.

Anonymous

Rolls Royce

"Beauty is truth, truth beauty,"—that is all
Ye know on earth, and all ye need to know.

John Keats

Mathematics possesses not only truth, but supreme beauty.

Bertrand Russell

"Joe, you're the most beautiful thing I ever saw."

Professional coach, on seeing his new
$400,000 quarterback

Is there any such thing as Absolute Beauty, which everyone will accept? Or is it merely personal—depending on birth, education, environment, and wishful thinking?

Do the images in this section tend to show that there is a single theme of beauty, with only small and agreeable variations? Or are there certain images here that dramatically contradict the others, suggesting irreconcilable kinds of beauty?

It may be that, as the metal "thing" on page 184 suggests, artists are in the process of showing us new kinds of beauty that some may find distasteful. In fifty years, dictionaries will have to throw out the old definitions and write new ones, not on the basis of tradition, but on what is actually being constructed. This kind of radical disturbance has already taken place around words like "morality" and "sex," and perhaps "beauty" will be one of the next to fall.

Or perhaps old beauties will still be recognized, but with new qualifications which will have to be accepted and which will thin out some of the intense preoccupation that used to be reserved to beauty. Maybe that is the significance of the sculpture—if it can be called that—on page 184.

This could mean that the newest art confirms an old saying: "Beauty is in the eye of the beholder."

Solid Geometry

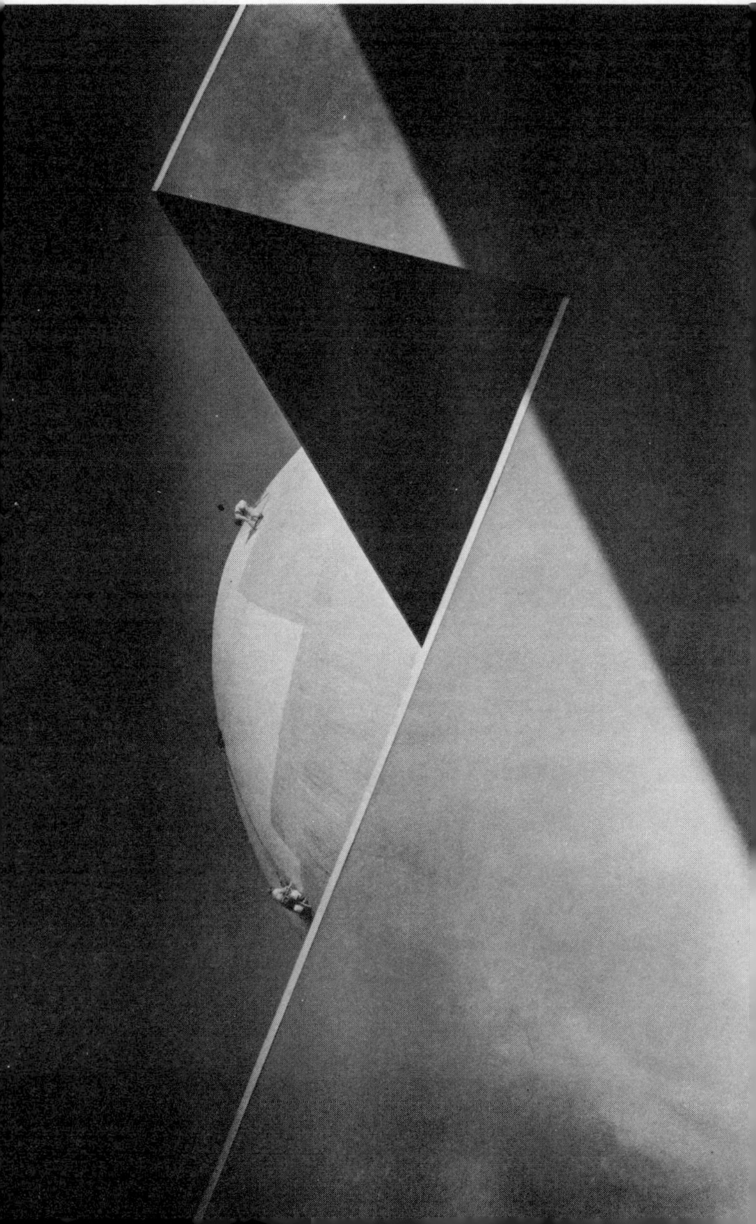

Greek Vase: Ajax and Achilles Playing Draughts

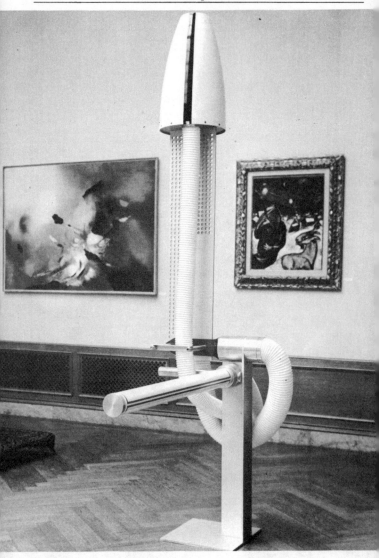

Exercises for writing:

1. Show how any one of the images fits any one of the definitions in the introduction.
2. Show how one image fits a different definition taken from some other source.
3. Can you make the "thing" on page 184 fit any idea of beauty?
4. Which two images are most obviously alike? Which two, though apparently dissimilar, really are much alike in their beauty?
5. Which one is closest to your own idea of beauty?
6. If none of them fit your ideas, find one that does and explain why.
7. Write a lyrical, highly emotional description of the beauty of one of these pictures.
8. Rewrite #7, with restraint.
9. Show how the idea of symmetry, or formal arrangement, adds to the beauty of any one image.
10. Pick an image from a different part of this book and show how it is related to the idea of beauty. Try to make a surprising choice.

Fourth Theme:
ABSTRACTION

*I do not wish to paint man as he is,
but as he might also have been . . . I do not paint my
contemporaries, I paint man and woman as
they are in legends. I only attach
myself to what is eternal. . . .
I attempt to show a man as an object, while
preserving the total purity
of line. Had I wished to show man as he is,
I should have needed such a confused
jumble of lines, that there could no longer have
been any question of elementary purity. . . .*

Paul Klee

The Boxers—Alexander Archipenko

Modern law and business schools require their students to study according to the "case system," in which individual situations—a crime, or a business failure—are analyzed in detail in order to find out the essential parts of each problem and to discover the general principles which govern each case.

In law school, the facts of the case, the testimony of witnesses, the lawyers' statements, and the judge's decision are studied, and then the student is required to make an "abstract" of one page, covering the most important parts of the whole conflict. What he does is to abstract, or draw out, only the most important elements, rigidly cutting away everything else. The process is very much like Madame Curie's discovery of radium, in which she had to sift 18,000 pounds of dirt in order to find the single speck of radioactive material that was sending out its signals through the mountain of mud and stones.

In abstract art, the same principle is at work, whether in photography, painting, or sculpture. Everything is ruthlessly eliminated that detracts from the one effect the artist wants to achieve. In his book on artistic perceptions, Bartlett Hayes describes it this way: "Artists have been increasingly interested in mass, space, movement and light and in the infinite ways these can be related without reference to what moves, what occupies the space, or what is illuminated."

The trouble for the observer is that such art immediately sets up a trembling conflict between what the observer expects to see when he reads the title, and what he actually sees. The boxers, for example, on the preceding page, do not look like expectable boxers, since everything has been abstracted except that one thing the artist wanted to convey.

Study the images in this section and be prepared to write about the CONTRAST between usual reality and the artistic interpretation.

Head—Alexei von Jawlensky

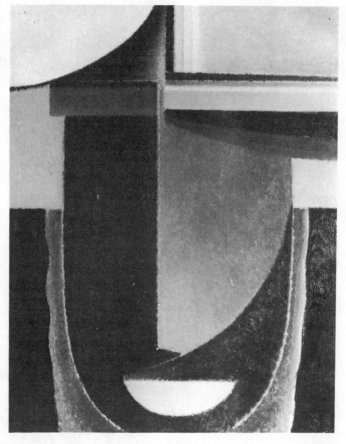

Horizontal Spines—Alexander Calder

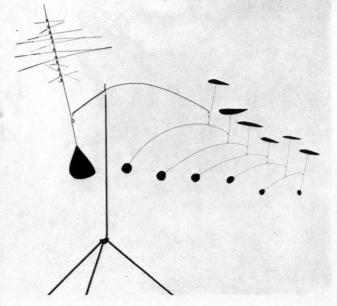

Model of the atomic arrangement of the myoglobin molecule

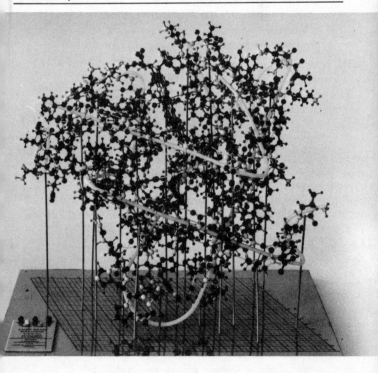

Exercises for ABSTRACTION:

1. Explain how one picture illustrates the contrast between artistic image and the usual reality.
2. Describe one abstraction in terms of what has been left out by the artistic treatment.
3. Can you explain how the abstract image reveals something which you never noticed about the reality?
4. Pick one of the images which appears to have little or no relation to any specific reality, and describe the effect of this isolation.
5. Describe one, or several, of the images in purely metaphorical terms.
6. Compare the two images on pages 190 and 191.
7. Pick a realistic incident—perhaps one you witnessed —and describe it in abstract terms. You might do this by imagining a realistic photograph, and then an abstract painting, drawing, or cartoon.
8. There is a tendency for abstract images to be monotonous. Can you explain what variations there are in one image in this section, one that might at first appear monotonous?
9. Describe one of these images in terms of shapes and forms, and the impressions they create.
10. Write a highly subjective description of just how one of these images makes you feel.

Fifth Theme:
AMBIGUITY

Do I dare to eat a peach?

T. S. Eliot, *The Love Song of J. Alfred Prufrock*

"*I'm going to be a computer when I grow up.*"

For some readers, the ambiguity of modern literature is annoying. They want straight, clear answers, right from the hip (not the hipster). They are like Charlie Brown: "I hate it when there are two sides to a question."

For others, ambiguity is a most fascinating part of reading or observing. They love to search for answers, as Madame Curie searched for radium, changing the course of the world by what she found. They love to argue back and forth from the two corners of ambiguity, matching strokes of emphasis to see which is stronger, therefore indicating the intent of the writer.

Most of all, these readers respond to what Robert Frost called the "tension" which is always present in a good line of poetry. This "good" quality comes from the tension of ambiguity; like a current flowing back and forth from one interpretation to another, it is the life-giving force in ambiguity.

What the unaccustomed reader dislikes is that this current creates a conflict of meanings. "Why didn't he make up his mind, and say *one* thing!" This is what many students ask when a conflict remains unsettled at the end of a play or story.

In studying the images in this section, analyze each one from the point of view of ambiguity, tension, and conflict. What elements are in opposition, both physical and intangible? Is there anything in the picture suggesting how the artist felt about the conflict—or ambiguity—he created? Are there hints as to a resolution of the tension?

Finally, consider how many ambiguities are suggested in each image, for some are complex and varied, demonstrating that the word "ambiguity" often means more than two uncertainties.

Relativity—M. C. Escher

Girl Before a Mirror—Picasso

Girl Before Her Mirror

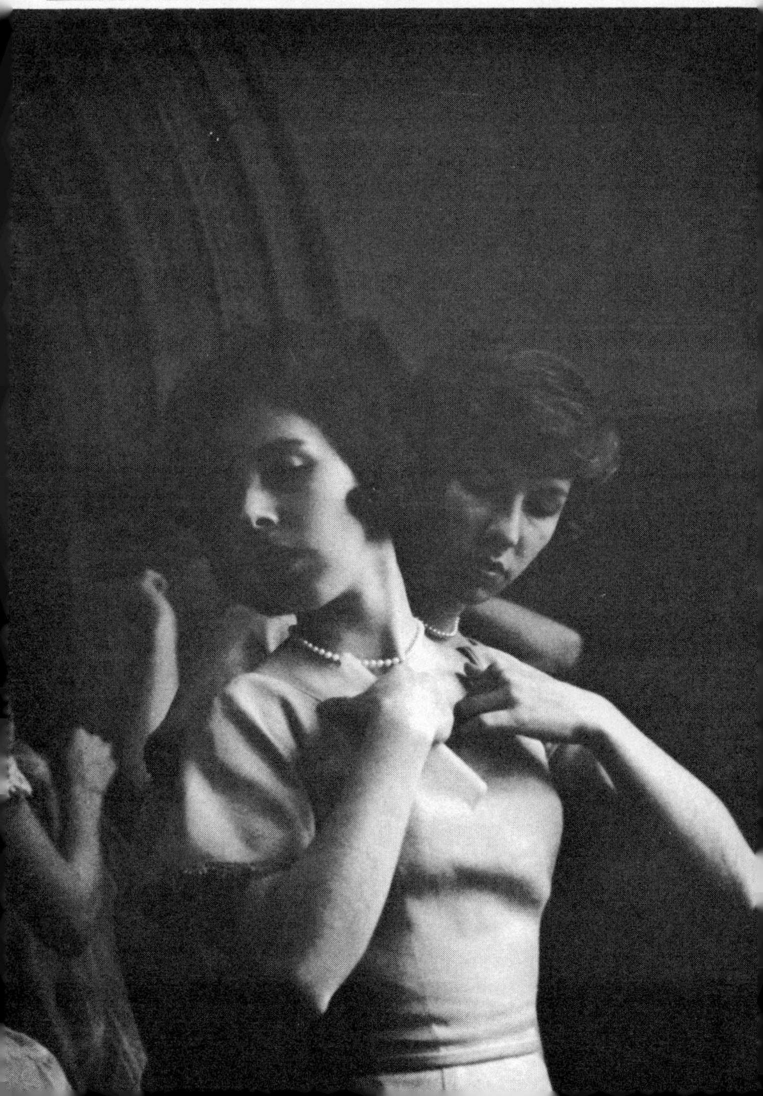

Advertisement for Automation

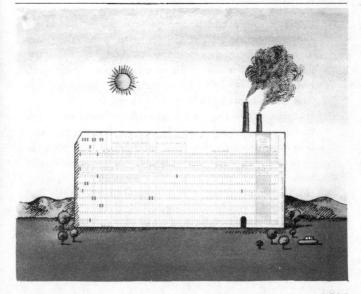

Exercises for AMBIGUITY:

1. Some of these individual pieces may not strike you as ambiguous at all, like the second one. If so, explain why you think it is so clear.
2. Which one do you consider most puzzling, most capable of a number of interpretations? Discuss these "meanings" in relation to each other.
3. Which one suggests the most contradictory ideas? Look up the word "paradox" and show that it does, or does not, fit any of the images.
4. Explain how the ambiguity in one image is similar to one you know of, either in art or literature or actual life.
5. Which one has the most uncomfortable tension? Why?
6. Using evidence from one picture, show on which side you think the artist's sympathies lie. One way of approaching this topic is to imagine what the picture would be like without one important element.
7. Explain an important similarity or difference between any two of the pairs of images.
8. Imagine a painting, photograph, or piece of sculpture that would be quite like one of those in this section, and describe it so that the similarity is clear to someone who can't see what is in your mental picture.
9. Do the same thing for a mental image quite the opposite of one in this section.
10. Find a classmate who has what you think is a completely false interpretation of one of these ambiguous pictures, and show what is wrong with his (or her) idea.

Sixth Theme:
CREATION

*From things that have happened and
from things as they exist and from all things
that you know and all those you cannot
know, you make something through
your invention that is not a
representation but a whole new thing
truer than anything true and alive,
and you make it alive, and if you make it
well enough, you give it immortality.*

Ernest Hemingway

God, the Creator—William Blake

The images in this section represent man's desire to make something new and different. It is a desire as old as man.

Genuine creation involves change and addition . . . or making something out of nothing . . . or rearranging old things into new combinations. Sometimes it presents old and familiar things in such a new way that it reveals a startling attitude or quality, with the result that the old can never again be what it was.

But the urge to create is always fighting against a different urge: to copy and repeat. There are many "artists" and observers who are perfectly happy to remain comfortably surrounded by things familiar and known. They dislike and distrust anything new and different— like modern dances and far-out movies—just because they are new and different. These people are not really involved in creative activity at all.

The same point can be made about newspaper reporting. Since its purpose is to repeat in words what has happened in the world of events, it is not a creative act. If it is as genuinely accurate and faithful as it is supposed to be, it does not change the form and character of what it reports.

By contrast, like some of the images in this section, creative writing attempts to invent new pictures, new characters, new events, new moments, all of which are made up in the mind of the writer. This is quite different from explaining an idea from a book, or answering questions on a history exam. And a student short story which is primarily mechanical narration of something that happened to the writer, is not really creative, either. It is reporting dressed up to look like something which it isn't.

Study each image in this section from the point of view of how new it is. Has the painter, or sculptor, really created something that did not exist before? Or has he added something new to what is perfectly recognizable? In other words, what are the essential characteristics of the "thing" he has made up?

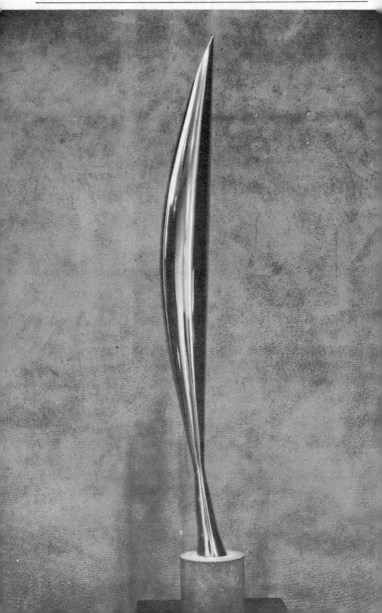

The Starry Night—Van Gogh

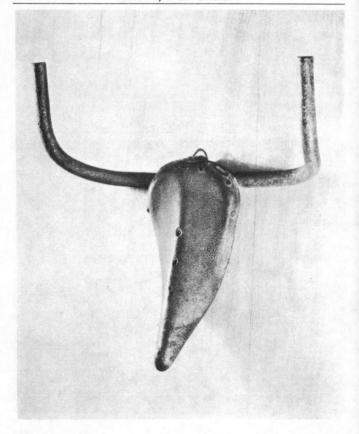

Southern Landscape—William Gropper

Exercises for CREATION theme:

1. For you, which of these creations presents the newest and most different mental picture? Describe what the artist has invented, in contrast to other things of the same kind which are by mere "copycats."
2. Describe your own personal, subjective feelings about the subject on page 209.
3. Which of these images is least creative, is more a re-arrangement of familiar things? Justify your opinion.
4. Select one of these "creations" which would probably be disliked because of its newness, and see if you can figure out what really lies behind the distaste. Explain this underlying reason, in contrast to what people might say out loud.
5. Try creating an idea of your own for a painting, sculpture, or photograph, and describe it in verbal terms as best you can. Decide what you would like your creation to "say."
6. Go back through other sections of the book and see if you can find an image which is in sharp contrast or comparison with one in this section. Explain the relationship from the point of view of creativeness.

Post-Test

Go back to the beginning and study the two pairs of images in the preliminary test. Write two new compositions of comparison, and then study them in relation to the first ones you wrote.

There are two major points of composition to consider: Is there any fundamental difference in the kind of subject matter you chose to write on? And is there any real distinction in the way you wrote—in choice of words, in the relationship of the parts to the whole (in sentences and paragraphs), and in the literary purpose of the compositions (narrative, descriptive, expository, argumentative)?

"Kind" of subjective matter means the quantity and vitality and significance of the details you observe; the importance of the relationships, both within an image and between two images; and the essence of what you really have to say about the images.

When you have finished this assignment, turn to the following final pair of pictures, and go through the same process of studying, comparing, and composing. Can you actually prove to yourself that you have observed MORE, and MORE SIGNIFICANTLY than when you started through this book?

One way to find out is to take one of your first papers and one of the last and write out your own careful analysis of the difference, both in subject matter and style. You might also ask someone else to do the same comparison.

Knee Bend Figure—Frank Gallo

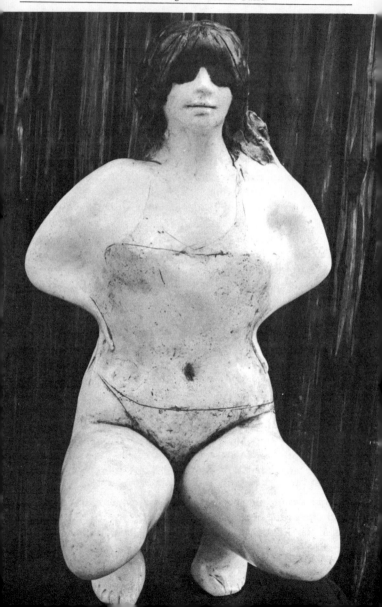

Draft Age—Jamie Wyeth

Conclusion

One of the greatest aims of education is to produce students who are able and willing to go on learning for the rest of their lives.

Some people are born with this capacity, and they continue to extend themselves despite all obstacles. Others must first learn and then develop a technique that will sustain them into middle and old age; or else on the day they graduate they will stop dead, and never learn another new thing unless it makes money.

The pictures and text in this book are just a beginning. There are thousands of other photographs, paintings, drawings, advertisements, cartoons, and sculptured figures which you have never seen or heard of before. There is undoubtedly a work of art being created right now, somewhere, that will be more surprising than anything in this entire book. It may be highly abstract or imaginative—perhaps even a new kind of art altogether—without any necessary or obvious connection with actual experience. It may require new principles of observation and understanding, above and beyond those emphasized in this book. It will certainly require some degree of tolerance.

The chances are, however, that any "new" art, or form of art, will still be the result of the artist's response to his environment. This is especially true of a writer, whether he is a student learning to extend and discipline his powers of observation or a professional who is trained in the process of seeing with feeling. Good writing is in a sense the result of observing with the eye and mind of an artist, so that what this book attempts to do, in part, is to provide a way to practice increasing the latent sense of artistry in all men.

The more this power increases, the more good subject matter it creates, which is the essence of all good talk and good writing.

Picture Credits

12 Louvre, Paris / 13 Margaret Bourke-White, LIFE Magazine © Time Inc. / 15 Hart Day Leavitt / 17 Johnny Florea, LIFE Magazine © Time Inc. / 19 Hugh Bell / 20 Prado, Madrid / 21 Academy of Motion Picture Arts and Sciences / 22 U.S. Army Photograph / 23 Charles Dana Gibson, Courtesy Langhorne Gibson / 24 Sheldon Brody / 25 Reproduced in the Unesco Art Popularization Series (1954) by the N.Y. Graphic Society, by arrangement with Unesco / 27 National Gallery of Art, Washington, D.C. / 29 Charles M. Schulz, United Feature Syndicate, copyright 1956 / 30 Anthony Bernato, United Press International photo / 31 By Permission of Her Majesty Queen Elizabeth II / 32 Wide World Photos / 34 Boston Museum of Fine Arts / 35 15th Cent. Flemish Painting, Boston Museum of Fine Arts / 37 Charles M. Schulz United Feature Syndicate, copyright 1963 / 39 Stadelsches Kunstinstitut, Frankfort am Main / 40 Carroll Seghers, II / 41 Cleveland Museum of Art, Mr. and Mrs. William H. Marlatt Fund / 42 Canadian Arena Co. / 43 Wallraf Richartz Museum, Cologne / 44 Dick Falcon / 47 The Art Institute of Chicago / 49 Museum of Fine Arts, Ghent / 50 Leavitt / 51 Gordon Bensley / 52 Harold Feinstein / 53 Pennsylvania Academy of the Fine Arts / 54 Capodimonte Museum, Naples / 55 Leavitt / 57 Whitney Museum of American Art / 59 Henk Jonker / 60 Bibliotheque Nationale, Paris / 61 Alte Pinakothek, Munich / 62 David Rubinger, copyright Time Inc. / 63 Museum of Modern Art Film Stills Archive / 64 Louvre / 65 William C. Shrout, LIFE Magazine © Time Inc. / 69 U.S. Instantaneous Photo Co., Library of Congress / 70 Portraits, Inc., N.Y. / 71 The Art Institute of Chicago / 72 H. Martin, Courtesy, *Saturday Review* / 73 Hermitage, Leningrad / 74 Elsbeth Siegrist, Virginia Museum of Fine Arts, Richmond, Va. / 75 Museum of Modern Art / 77 Charles M. Schulz, United Feature Syndicate, copyright 1957 / 79 Robert Kelley, LIFE Magazine © Time Inc. / 80 Leavitt / 81 Kunsthistorischen Museum, Vienna / 82 Charles Addams, *The New Yorker Magazine* / 83 Collection C. V. S. Roosevelt, Washington, D.C. / 84 Prado, Madrid / 85 *Boston Record American* / 87 *Saturday Review* / 89 Guy Gillette / 90 Bob Willoughby, from LEE GROSS / 91 National Gallery of Art, Washington, D.C., Rosenwald Collection / 92 International Atomic Energy Laboratory, Vienna / 93 Jakob Tuggener / 94 Louvre / 95 Robert Frank / 97 Joseph J. Scherschel, LIFE Magazine © Time Inc. / 100 The Art Institute of Chicago / 101 *The New York Times* / 102 Addison Gallery of American Art, Andover, Mass. / 103 Carola Rust / 104 Yasushi Nagao, United Press International photo / 105 Alte Pinakothek, Munich / 109 Royal Fine Arts Museum, Antwerp / 110 Rolf Nelson Gallery, Los Angeles / 111 Browne-Vintners Co., New York / 112 Robert Frank / 113 Ronald Searle from *Haven't We Met Before Somewhere* by Ronald Searle and Heinz Huber, The

Picture Credits

Viking Press / 114 Leavitt / 115 Georg Oddner / 117 Stephen Trefonides, Museum of Fine Arts, Boston / 119 Arne Andersson / 120 Richard Amu / 121 Kunstmuseum, Basel / 122 Inge Morath, MAGNUM / 123 Greek Sculpture, 2nd Century B.C., Metropolitan Museum of Art, Rogers Fund / 124 National Gallery of Scotland, on loan from the Duke of Sutherland / 125 Richard Avedon / 129 Herbert Goldberg / 130 Museum of Modern Art / 131 Tim Kantor, *The New York Times* / 132 *Gemini 7*, NASA Photo from UPI / 133 M. Knoedler & Co., N.Y. / 134 Gallerie Chelette, New York / 135 Avco Corporation / 137 *Saturday Review* / 139 Museum of Modern Art / 140 French Government Tourist Office / 141 Eliot Elisofon, LIFE Magazine © Time Inc. / 142 Martin J. Dain, SCOPE Associates / 144 Whitney Museum of American Art / 145 from *The New Architecture of Europe*, by G. E. Kidder Smith, Photo Durand-Pyrebesse, Paris / 147 U.S. Army Photograph / 149 Rijksmuseum, Amsterdam / 150 Library of Congress / 151 Museum of Fine Arts, Boston, Francis Welch Fund / 152 Picasso, Museum of Modern Art / 153 Herbert Block, from *Straight Herblock*, Simon & Schuster, 1964 / 154 Lockheed Aircraft Corporation / 155 Jack Eckert, *N.Y. Daily News Photo* / 159 Dresden Art Gallery / 160 Robert Frank / 161 Prado / 162 Unknown German Photographer, Museum of Modern Art / 163 I. Wilmer Counts / 164 Lynn Pelham, Rapho-Guillumette, LIFE Magazine © Time Inc. / 165 LIFE Magazine © Time Inc. / 169 Sidney Janis Gallery, Photo by John D. Schiff / 170 DeWayne Dalrymple / 171 Leavitt / 172 Philadelphia Museum of Art / 173 *The New Yorker* / 174 Collection of Henry Torczyner, New York, Photo by G. D. Hackett / 179 Ben Schnall / 180 Berlin State Museum, Photo by Walter Steinkopf / 181 Philadelphia Museum of Art, Photo by A. J. Wyatt / 182 Allinari, Art Reference Bureau / 183 Alfred Eisenstaedt, LIFE Magazine © Time Inc. / 184 Dilexi Gallery, San Francisco / 185 Dmitri Kessel, LIFE Magazine © Time Inc. / 187 The Bettmann Archive / 189 Redfern Gallery, London / 190 Leavitt / 191 Collection Mr. and Mrs. Max M. Zurier, Los Angeles / 192 New York State Historical Association / 193 Addison Gallery of Art, Andover, Mass. / 194 Addison Gallery / 195 from Penguin Science Survey, 1961 / 197 Courtesy Mrs. James Thurber / 199 Charles M. Schulz, United Feature Syndicate / 200 Museum of Modern Art / 201 Museum of Modern Art / 202 Museum of Modern Art / 203 Leavitt / 204 The Brooklyn Museum / 205 General Telephone & Electronics / 207 Whitworth Art Gallery, Manchester, England / 209 Federal Court House, Newark, New Jersey / 210 Museum of Modern Art / 211 Museum of Modern Art / 212 Tudor Publishing Co. / 213 San Francisco Art Institute / 214 French Embassy Press and Information Division / 218 Graham Gallery, New York / 219 Photo by Lee Bolton, Time-Life Books / 220 National Gallery, London / 221 Rolf Winquist